Date

Dear

From

Blessings of Hope

© 2005 by Roy Lessin

© 2005 Christian Art Gifts, RSA
        Christian Art Gifts Inc., IL, USA

First edition 2005
Second edition 2012

Images used under license from Shutterstock.com

Designed by Christian Art Gifts

Printed in China

ISBN 978-1-77036-750-0

13   14   15   16   17   18   19   20   21   22   –   11   10   9   8   7   6   5   4   3   2

BLESSINGS
OF HOPE

ROY LESSIN

christian
art gifts®

Contents

Spiritual blessings

God is concerned about your well-being, both physically and spiritually. He wants you to prosper and be in health, even as your soul prospers (see 3 John 1:2).

Above all, He wants you to be a spiritually healthy person.

Spiritual blessings are the greatest blessings you can receive. The Bible tells us that every spiritual blessing is ours in Jesus Christ.

The Source of our blessings

"Blessed be the God and Father of our
Lord Jesus Christ, who has blessed us
with every spiritual blessing
in the heavenly places in Christ."

Ephesians 1:3, NKJV

Jesus is not only the Source of our spiritual blessings, but He is the spiritual blessing that we hunger for in our lives. In Jesus Christ, everything you receive will bring you spiritual health. You can freely receive and enjoy every good and perfect gift that is in His heart to give you.

He wants to bless you

You can receive **peace,**

for He is the Prince of Peace;

wisdom, for He is the Counselor;

hope, for He is the Alpha and Omega;

rest, for He is the Good Shepherd;

truth, for He is the Word of God;

courage, for He is the Mighty God;

cleansing, for He is the Lamb of God;

righteousness, for He is the Righteous One.

There is so much that He wants
to bless you with today.

"The Lord bless you and keep you;
the Lord make His face shine
upon you, and be gracious to you;
the Lord lift up His countenance
upon you, and give you peace."

Numbers 6:24-26, NKJV

An abundance of blessings

The source of the blessing given in Numbers 6:24-26 is God alone. Everything in this blessing is God's perfect will for you. It comes directly from His heart to touch your life.

It is a blessing that is right for you, needful for you, and best for you. It is God giving you the highest, the richest, and the fullest measure of His goodness.

It is a blessing that He wants to pour upon you in abundance so that you will never lack His supply.

It is a blessing that keeps you under His protective care and covering; that causes His favor to rest upon you; that fills your heart with love and shines out through your countenance; that gives you, moment-by-moment, every grace you need to do His will and fulfill His purpose for you.

God's blessing brings His smile over your life as He cares for you, provides for you, and encourages you with His presence.

He touches the deepest part of your spirit with a peace that calms every storm, heals every wound, and comforts you in every trial.

The blessing of "Shalom"

"Then Gideon built an altar there unto the Lord,
and called it Jehovah-shalom."

Judges 6:24, KJV

When we greet someone we usually say "hello," and when we leave we usually say "goodbye." It is a nice social greeting, but it has no deep or profound meaning behind it.

In Israel, however, when you greet someone or say goodbye, the word that is used is "Shalom." "Shalom" is much more than a casual social greeting – it is a prayer, a blessing, a desire, and a benediction. It is a word that is packed with the full benefits of God's favor.

In Hebrew the word *"shalom"* has many significant meanings throughout the Scriptures. The following blessing is a compilation of those meanings.

May you be whole in body, soul, and spirit
as a result of being in harmony
with God's will and purpose for your life.

May His peace be your covering,
your heart know His fullness,
and by His mighty power may you know victory
over every enemy. May He bring to pass
the deepest desires of your heart ...

May you know the healing power of His presence,
and the restoration of every broken relationship.
Through His sufficiency, may His limitless resources
meet every need that you face.

May His covenant promises be fulfilled
in your life and in your family.
May He bring you the greatest measure
of contentment and the deepest satisfaction
that your heart can possibly know.

"Lord, You establish
peace for us;
all that we have
accomplished
You have done for us."

Isaiah 26:12

Be a blessing to others

"I will bless you ... and you will be a blessing."

Genesis 12:2

One of the reasons God has blessed
your life is because He wants you
to be a blessing to others.
The rivers of living water
that flow into your heart
are meant to flow out to others.
His forgiveness in your life
releases you to forgive others.
His mercies in your life
enable you to extend mercy to others.
It is His kindness that makes you kind,
His grace that makes you gracious,
and His generosity that makes you generous.

A harvest of blessings

The harvest of good things that He has produced in you also provides the seeds that allow you to sow into the lives of others.

"Now He who supplies seed to the
sower and bread for food will also supply
and increase your store of seed and will
enlarge the harvest of your righteousness.
You will be made rich in every way
so that you can be generous on every
occasion, and through us your generosity
will result in thanksgiving to God."

2 Corinthians 9:10-11

The Lord is always near you

What could be sweeter or dearer than to know
that no one is nearer to your heart, your soul,
or your deepest desires than the Lord?

His caring eyes are upon you.

His loving heart responds to you.

You can come to Him in quietness and confidence,
in faith, in hope, in trust, in thanks, in worship,
in praise, and in prayer.

"My voice shalt Thou hear
in the morning, O Lord;
in the morning will I
direct my prayer unto Thee,
and will look up."

Psalm 5:3, KJV

You are in good hands

He will give to you over and over again. Because His supply is abundant you will never be without ... because His heart is full you will never be empty ... because His resources are endless there will never be a time when He cannot meet your needs.

Your life couldn't be in better hands. As you come to Him in prayer remember how much He desires to bless you.

The quiet places God brings you to are rich with life and nourishment ... cool with delight and refreshing ... pleasant with freedom and beauty.

They are places of rest to quiet your heart ... places of hope to renew your spirit ... places of joy to delight your soul.

You are so blessed to be able to share the Lord's quiet company. It pleases His heart to hear your heart speak words of praise and thanks to Him.

He will bring you rest

In your quiet times or busy times God has a quiet place for you to rest. It is a place of still waters. His waters are present to wash you, delight you, and refresh you. He will bring you rest from all your fears, worries, cares, and anxieties. In His quiet place there is no weight upon you, no confusion around you, and no clouds over you. It is the place where you can peacefully open your heart to Him.

Come before the Lord

It is delightful to come before the Lord in quietness, in adoration, and in prayer. As you kneel at His feet and gaze upon His face, renewal gently comes. In your weariness you will be refreshed, in your weakness your strength will be renewed, in your heaviness your heart will sing a new song. His wings will be your covering, His faithfulness will be your shield, His lovingkindness will be your sweet reward. Beautiful are His ways with you.

The paths of prayer

As you walk the paths of prayer
you will be guided into everything
that is true and right ...
into all that is best for you and others ...
into all that will take you
to the highest expressions of His love.
He will lead you by His way,
by His words, and by His will.
He will guide you down the paths
that lead you straight to His heart.
Each prayer He answers
will be for your good and for His glory.

God is great

The greatest thing your heart can experience
when you are alone with God is His presence.
He is greater than any of His gifts.
What He is to you is greater
than anything He can do for you.
His lovingkindness is better than life ...
in His presence is fullness of joy ...
at His right hand are pleasures forevermore.
When God gives Himself to you there is
nothing higher that He can give.

Safe within God's care

Comfort in prayer comes by knowing that the One you look to is always looking out for you. He is not only with you, but He is actively doing everything that is necessary to keep you safe within His care.

You can be assured that above you are His tender mercies ... around you is His unfailing love ... and underneath you are His everlasting arms.

Even though you may have things that come against you, you have so much more going for you. While your enemies try to rob you of your joy, God spreads a lavish table before you filled with spiritual blessings of goodness, kindness, and love.

As you come to Him in prayer you find a table your soul can delight in ... your faith can feast upon ... and your heart can rejoice in.

When you come to God in times of personal dryness, when you are in need of help or healing, or when you are in a desert place, you will find His loving hand pouring out the oil of His Spirit upon you – comforting, refreshing, and filling you to overflowing.

His oil heals and soothes, calms and relieves, and causes your face to shine with the glow of His presence.

How glorious and wonderful are the things that follow you into prayer – kindness, beauty, goodness, mercy, grace, favor, blessings, faithfulness and lovingkindness. In His great generosity He has given to you freely, bountifully, cheerfully. He has given you the finest, the highest, the deepest, and the fullest measure of His love. All that He has given He will continue to give to you all the days of your life.

Your future is secure

Now you are a pilgrim with needs to be met and people to minister to along the way. One day you will be in your Father's house, the need for asking will have passed away and only praise will remain. In Jesus, your future is secure and your destiny certain. Today is the time to bring before Him all those who, like you, are in need of hope and encouragement on their journey home.

"In My Father's house are many mansions:
if it were not so, I would have told you.
I go to prepare a place for you.
And if I go and prepare a place for you,
I will come again, and receive you unto Myself;
that where I am, there ye may be also."

John 14:2-3, KJV

"His divine power has given to us

all things that pertain to life and godliness,

through the knowledge of Him who

called us by glory and virtue,

by which have been

given to us exceedingly

great and precious

promises."

2 Peter 1:3-4, NKJV

God keeps His promises

When people make promises and break them, it can be for various reasons.

One is that they never intended to keep the promise in the first place. Another reason is that they promised more than they were able to do. Another is that they had good intentions, but forgot the promise they made. Another is that they hadn't forgotten, but on the way to fulfilling the promise they got distracted and gave their attention to something else.

When God makes a promise to you He has every intention of fulfilling it, has the resources to fulfill it, will not forget to fulfill it, and He will not get distracted from fulfilling it.

Every promise that God has made to you in Christ is a "yes".

"Let us hold fast the confession
of our hope without wavering,
for He who promised is faithful."

Hebrews 10:23, NKJV

An expression of His love

Every promise of God is an extension of His will.
His faithfulness to His promises
is a reflection of His character. The fulfillment
of His promises is an expression of His love.
If God were to break His promises He would have to
denounce His word, defame His character, deny His love,
destroy His covenants, and discredit the work of His Son.
Such a thing is not only unthinkable but it is
also impossible because God cannot lie.

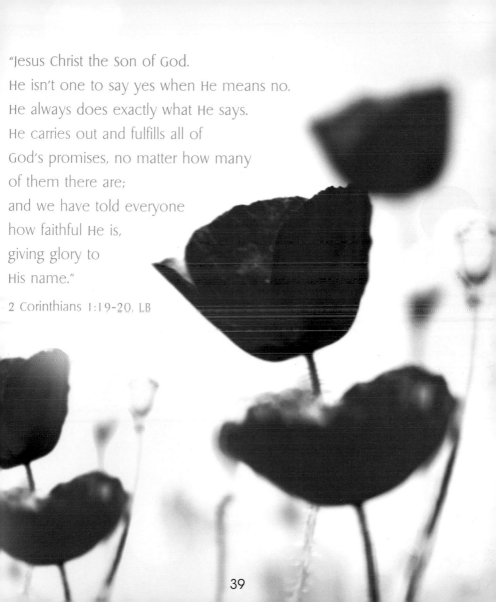

"Jesus Christ the Son of God.
He isn't one to say yes when He means no.
He always does exactly what He says.
He carries out and fulfills all of
God's promises, no matter how many
of them there are;
and we have told everyone
how faithful He is,
giving glory to
His name."

2 Corinthians 1:19-20, LB

"For men indeed swear
by the greater, and an oath
for confirmation is for them
an end of all dispute.
Thus God, determining to show
more abundantly to the heirs of
promise the immutability
of His counsel, confirmed it
by an oath, that by two
immutable things, in which it is
impossible for God to lie,
we might have strong consolation,
who have fled for refuge to lay hold
of the hope set before us."

Hebrews 6:16-18, NKJV

You in Him, He in you

Jesus has promised to be with you always. How close is He? His Spirit is joined to your spirit. He is closer than any person could ever be. He is in complete union with you – you are in Him and He is in you.

You are seated with Christ in heavenly places; nothing is higher than that. He loves you; nothing is deeper than that. He communes with you; nothing is sweeter than that.

He is with you; nothing is nearer than that. He is in you; nothing is closer than that. He has given you His promises; nothing is surer than that.

"He that dwelleth in the secret places
of the most High shall abide
under the shadow of the Almighty."

Psalm 91:1, KJV

Standing on God's promises

Standing on the promises that cannot fail,
when the howling storms of doubt and fear assail,
by the living word of God I shall prevail,
standing on the promises of God.

Standing on the promises I cannot fall,
listening every moment to the Spirit's call,
resting in my Savior as my all in all,
standing on the promises of God.

R. Kelso Carter

God's promises are amazing.
Expect the amazing,
because God does amazing things.

For the need you face there is
a promise God has spoken,
and with every promise God has spoken
there is a provision that has been made
to meet that need.

"For the Lord your God
will bless you
just as He promised you."

Deuteronomy 15:6, NKJV